SWEAR WORD COLORING BOOK
FOR ADULTS

THIS BOOK BELONGS TO

_____

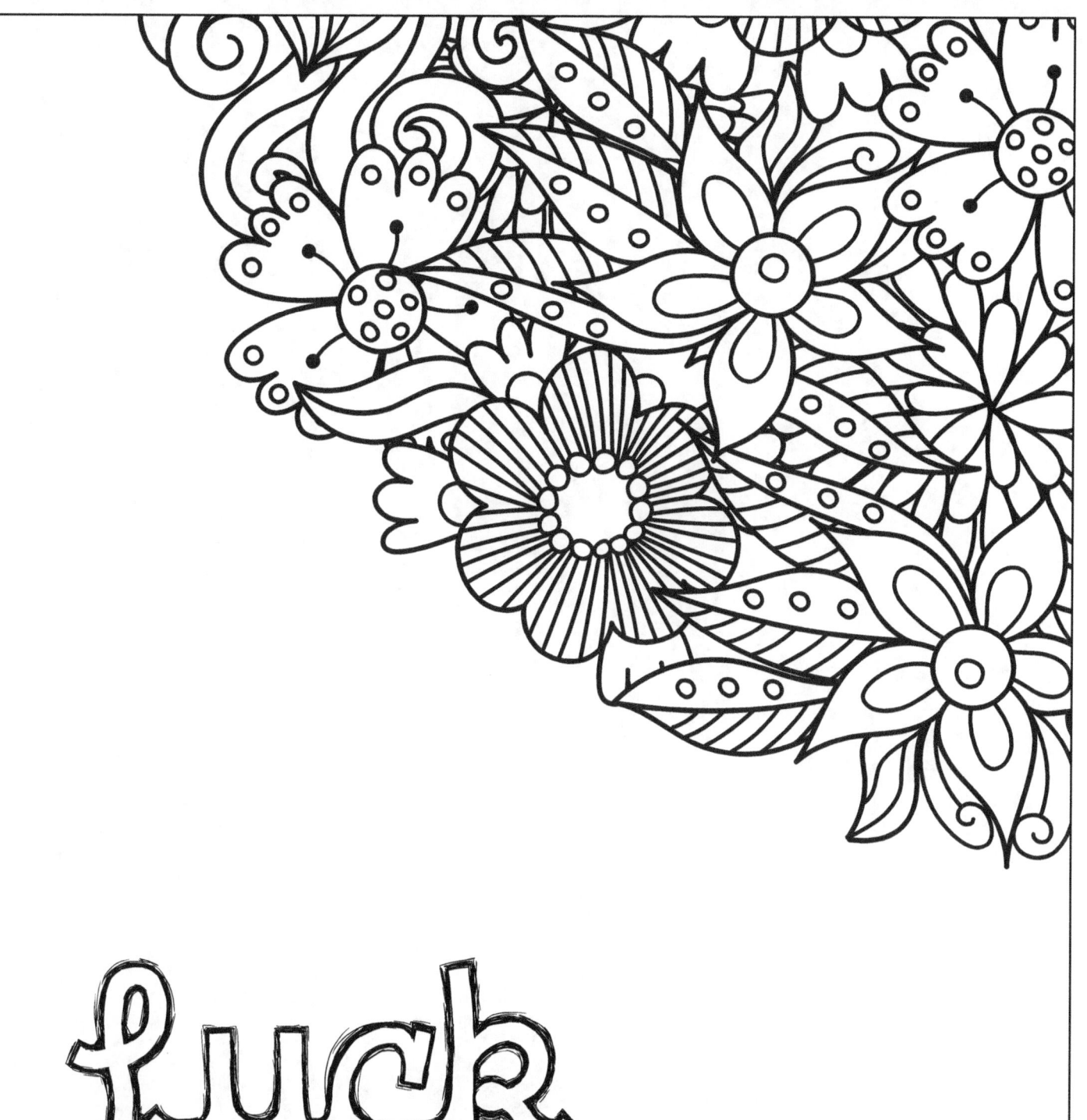

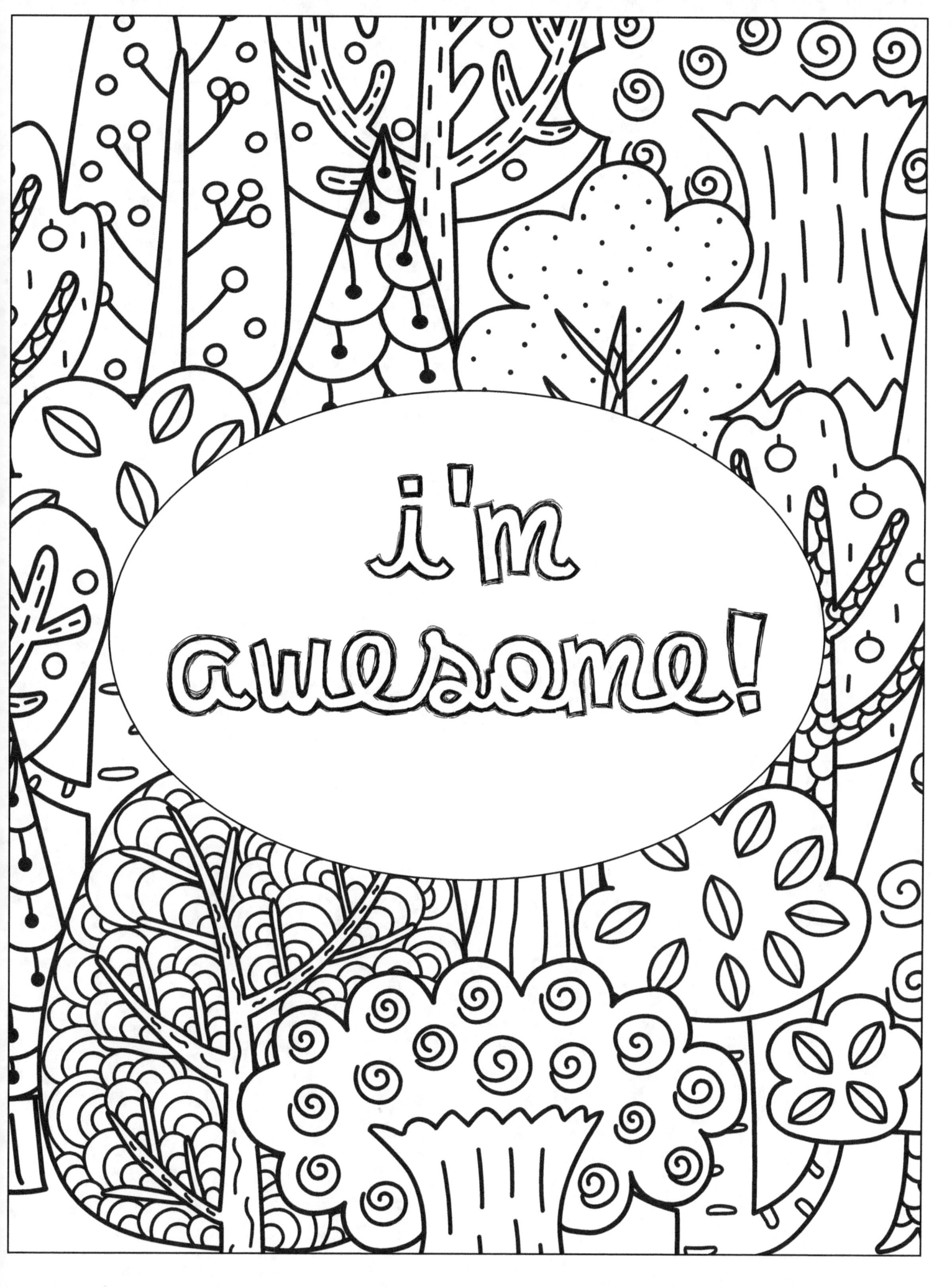

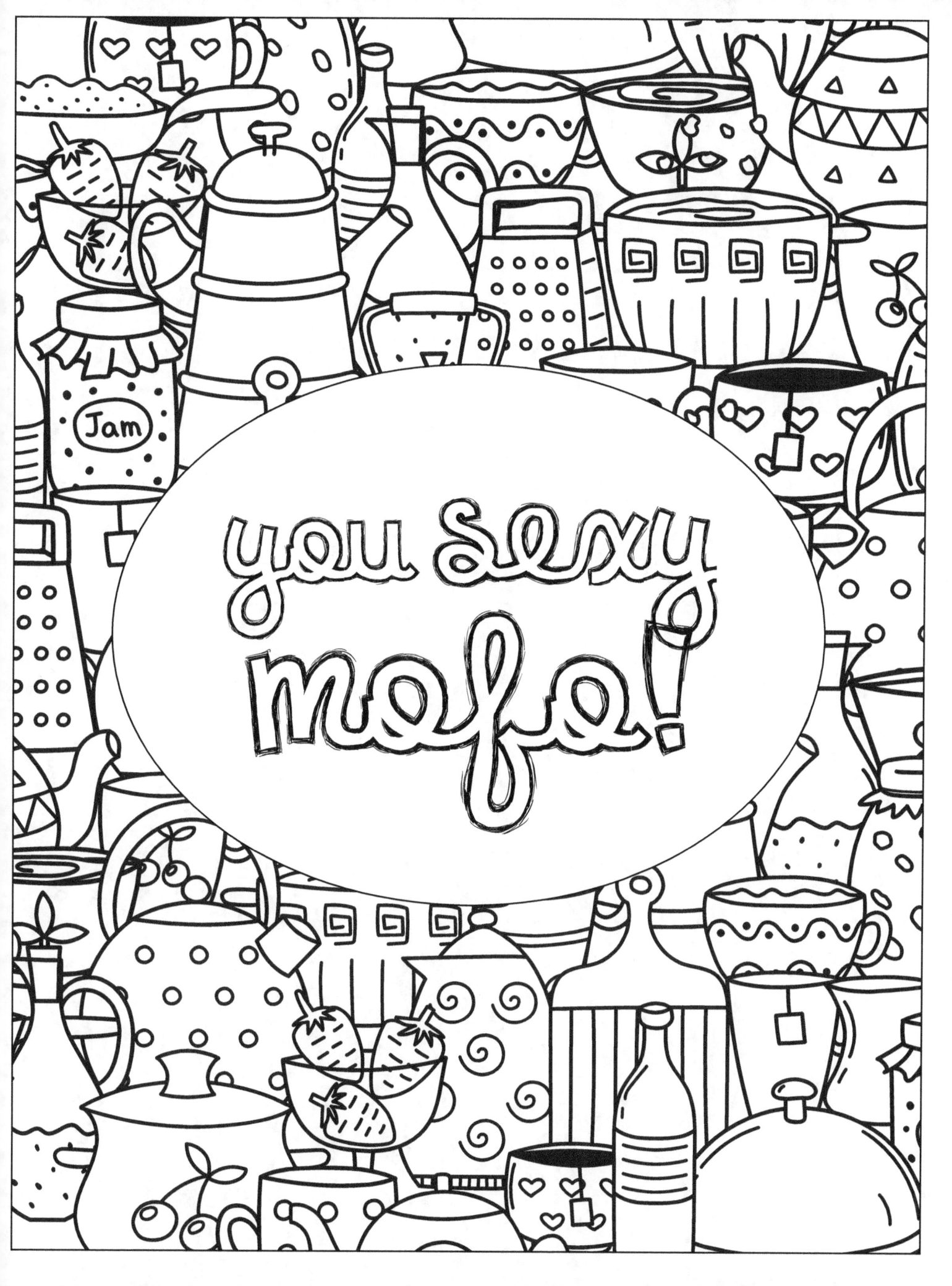

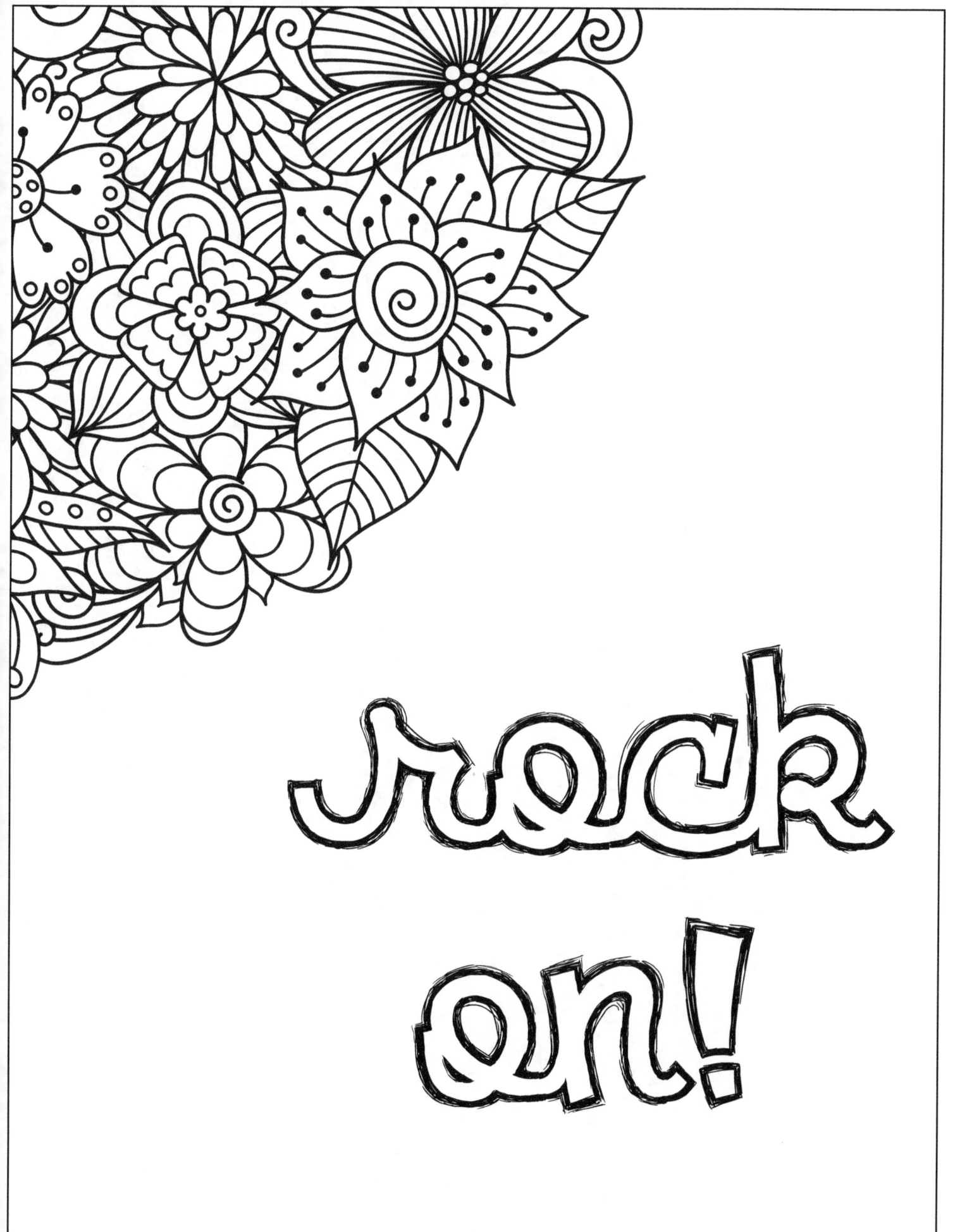

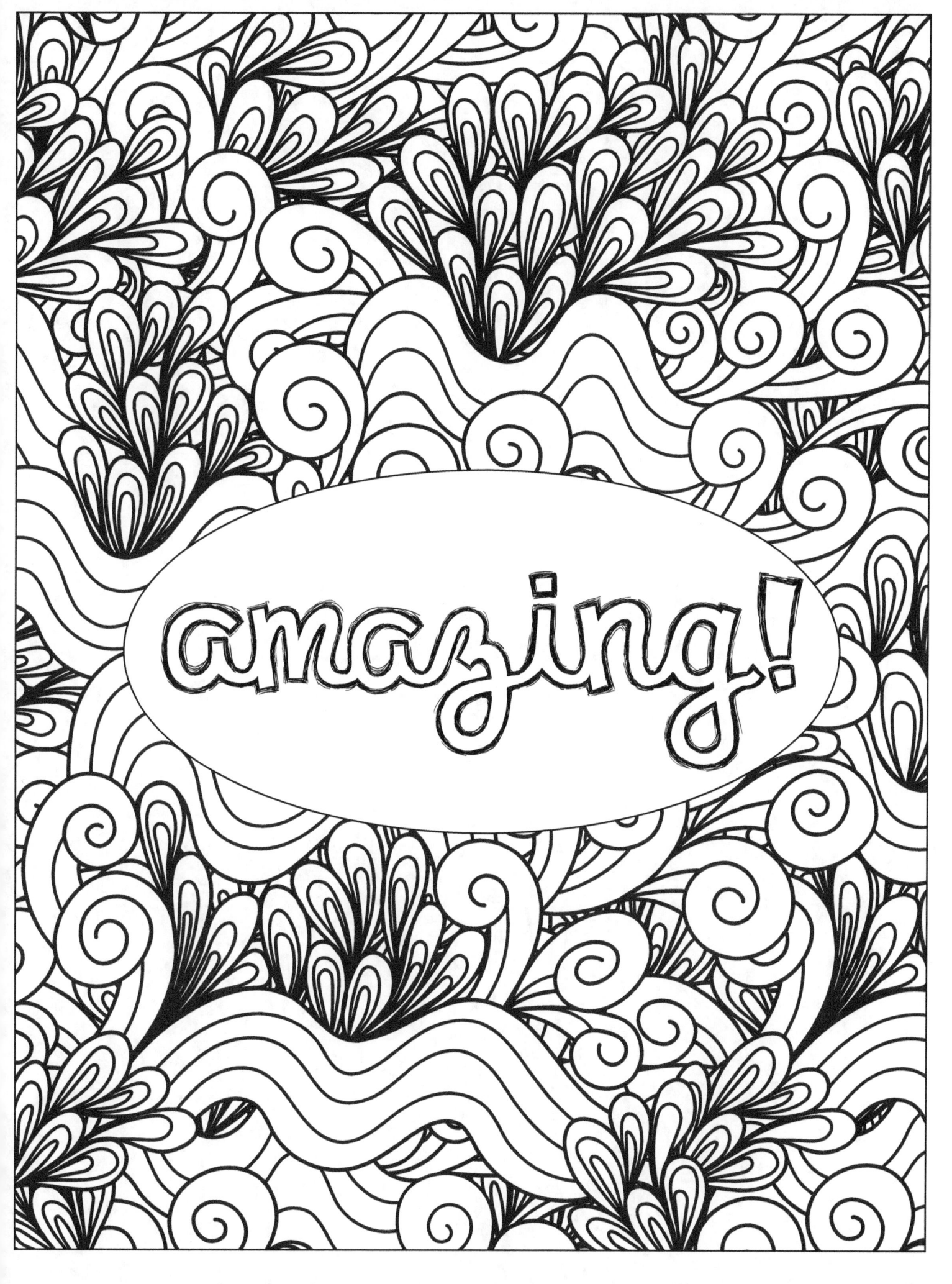

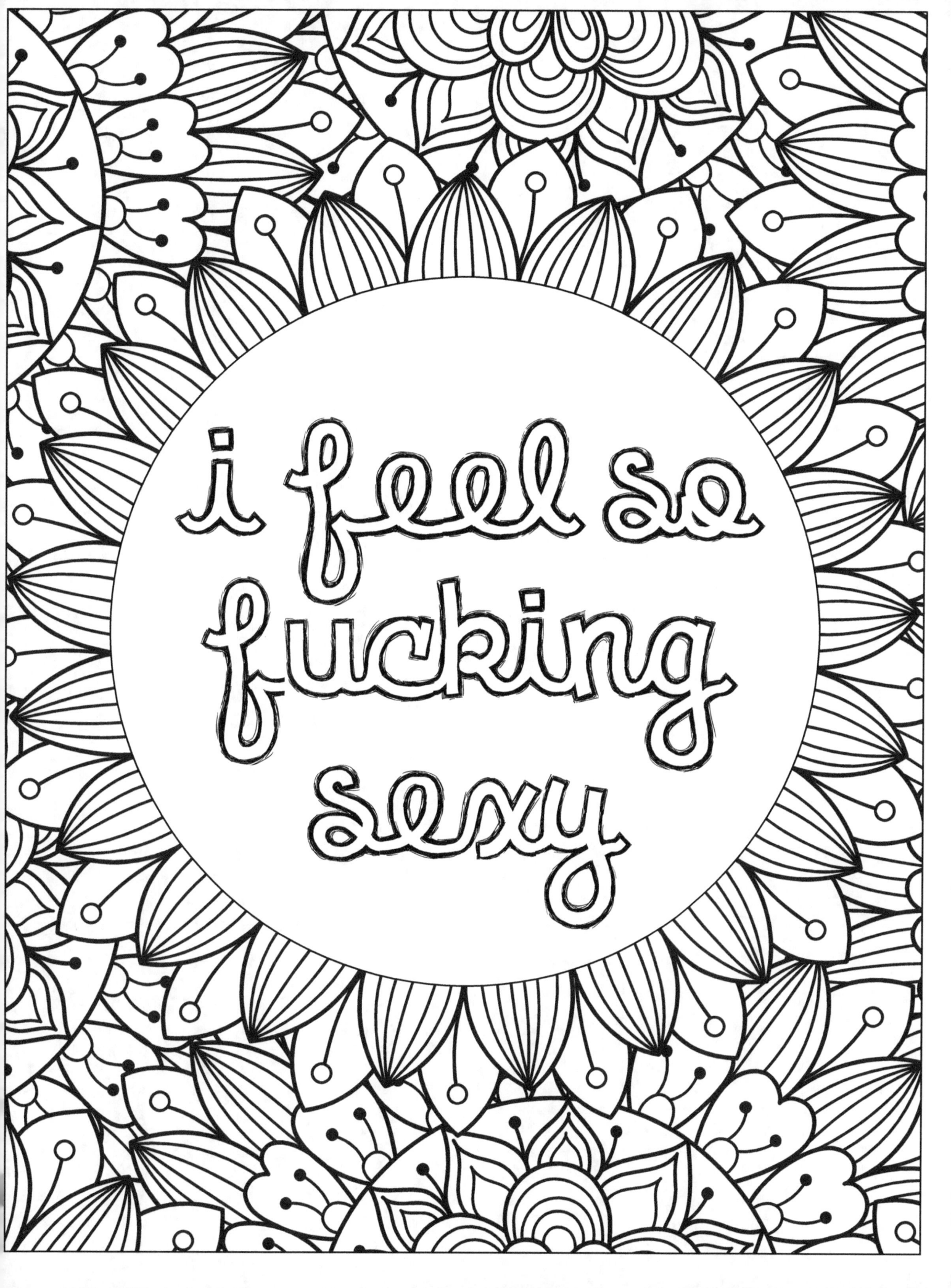

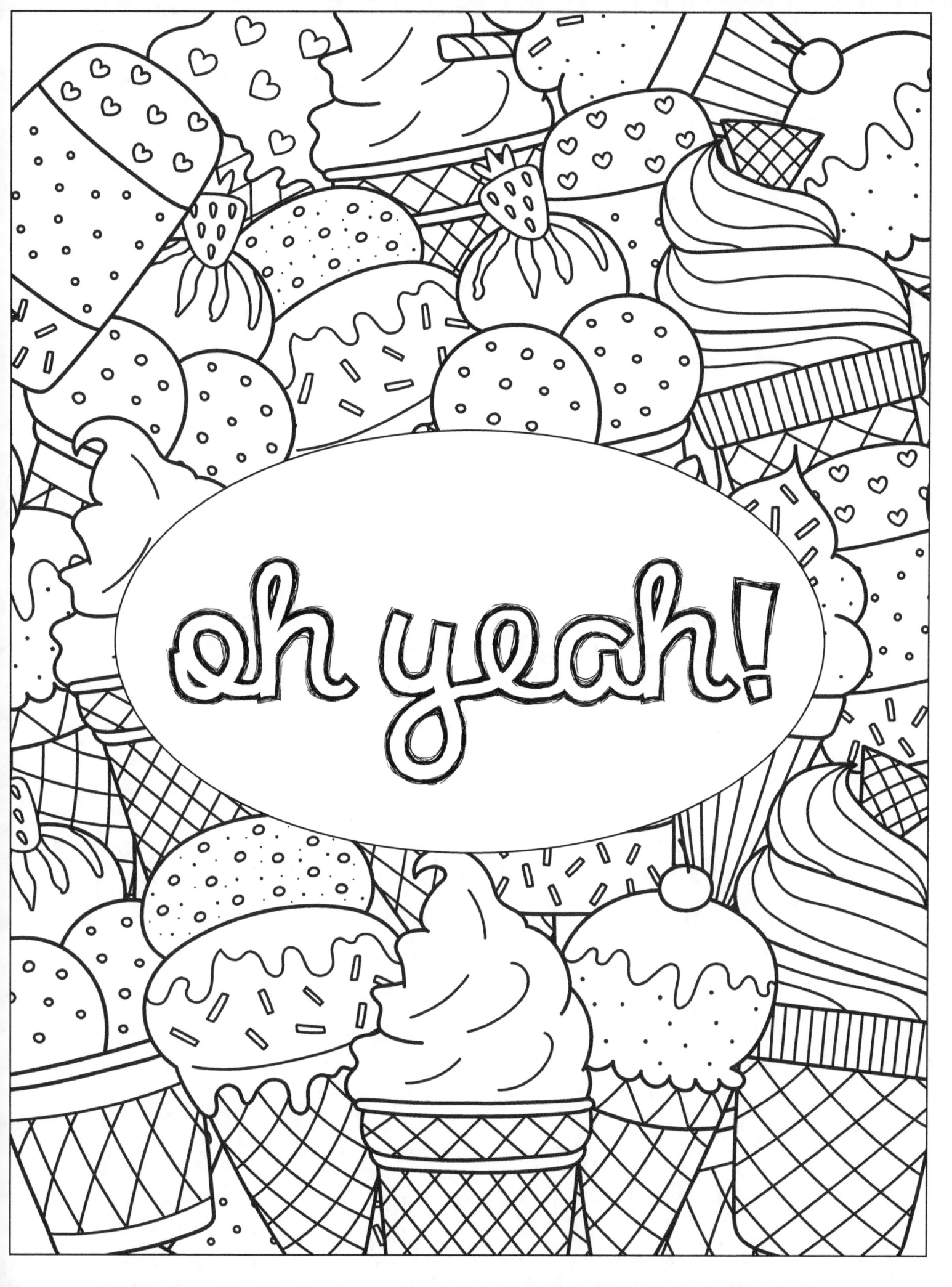

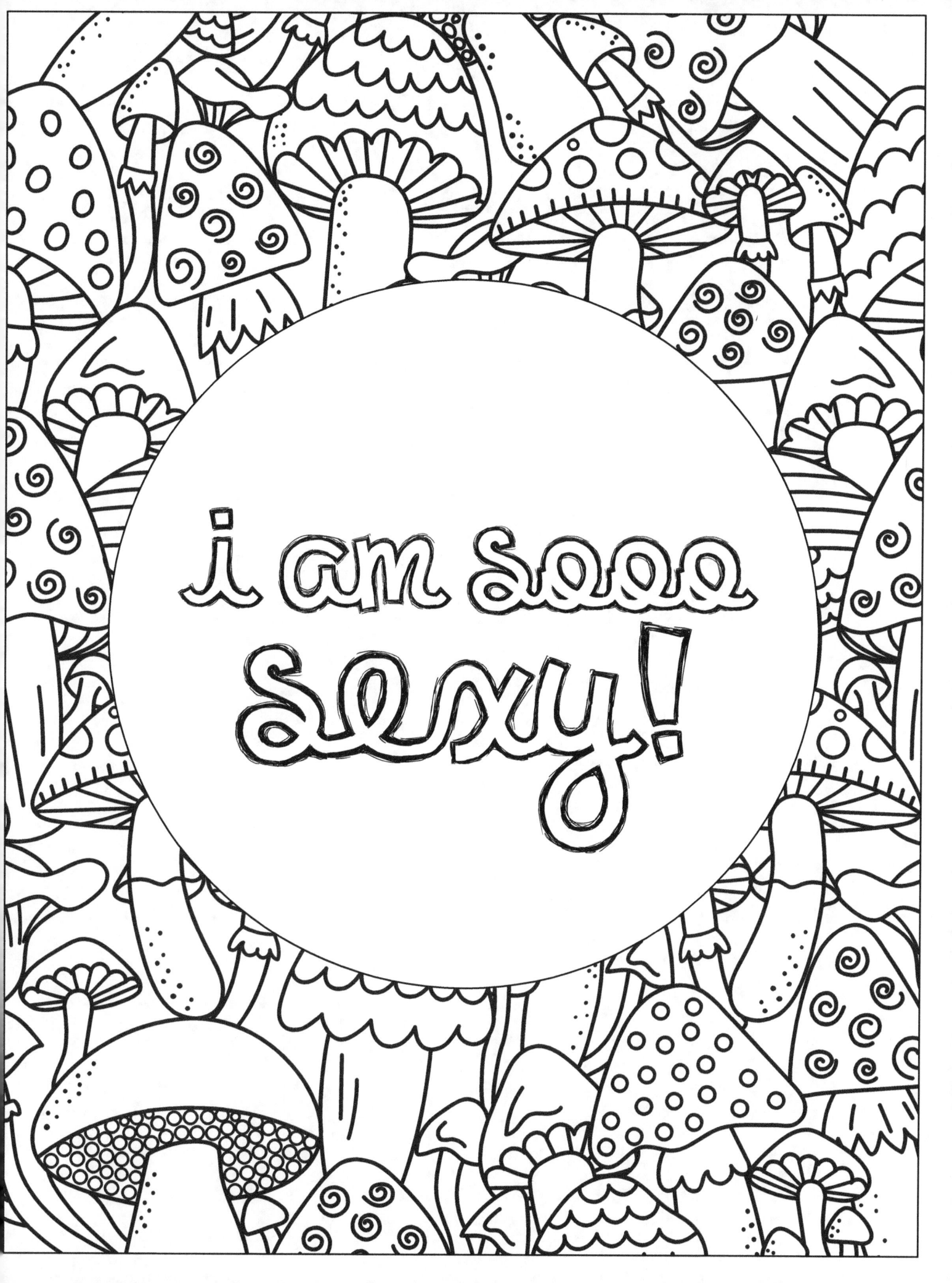

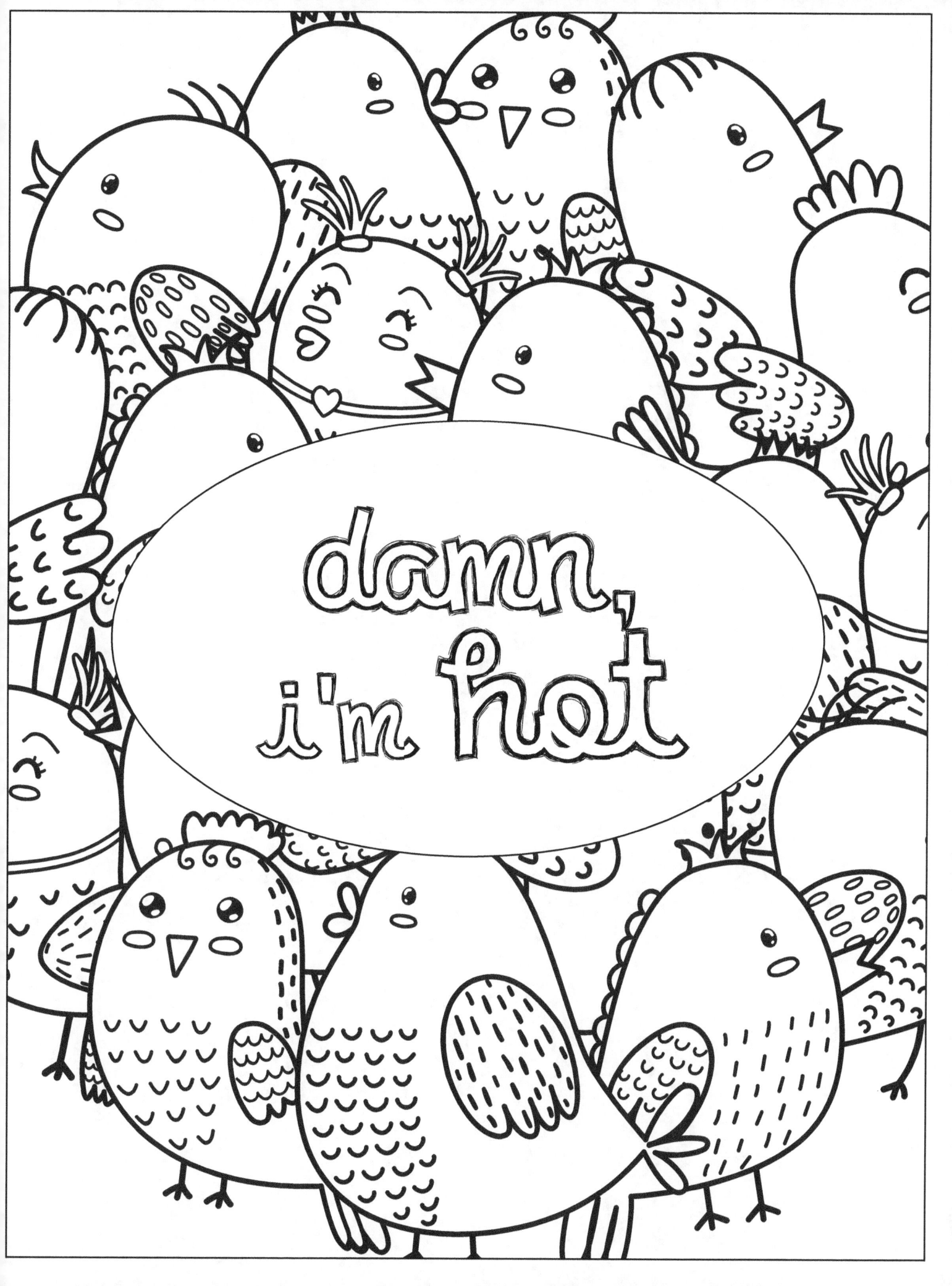

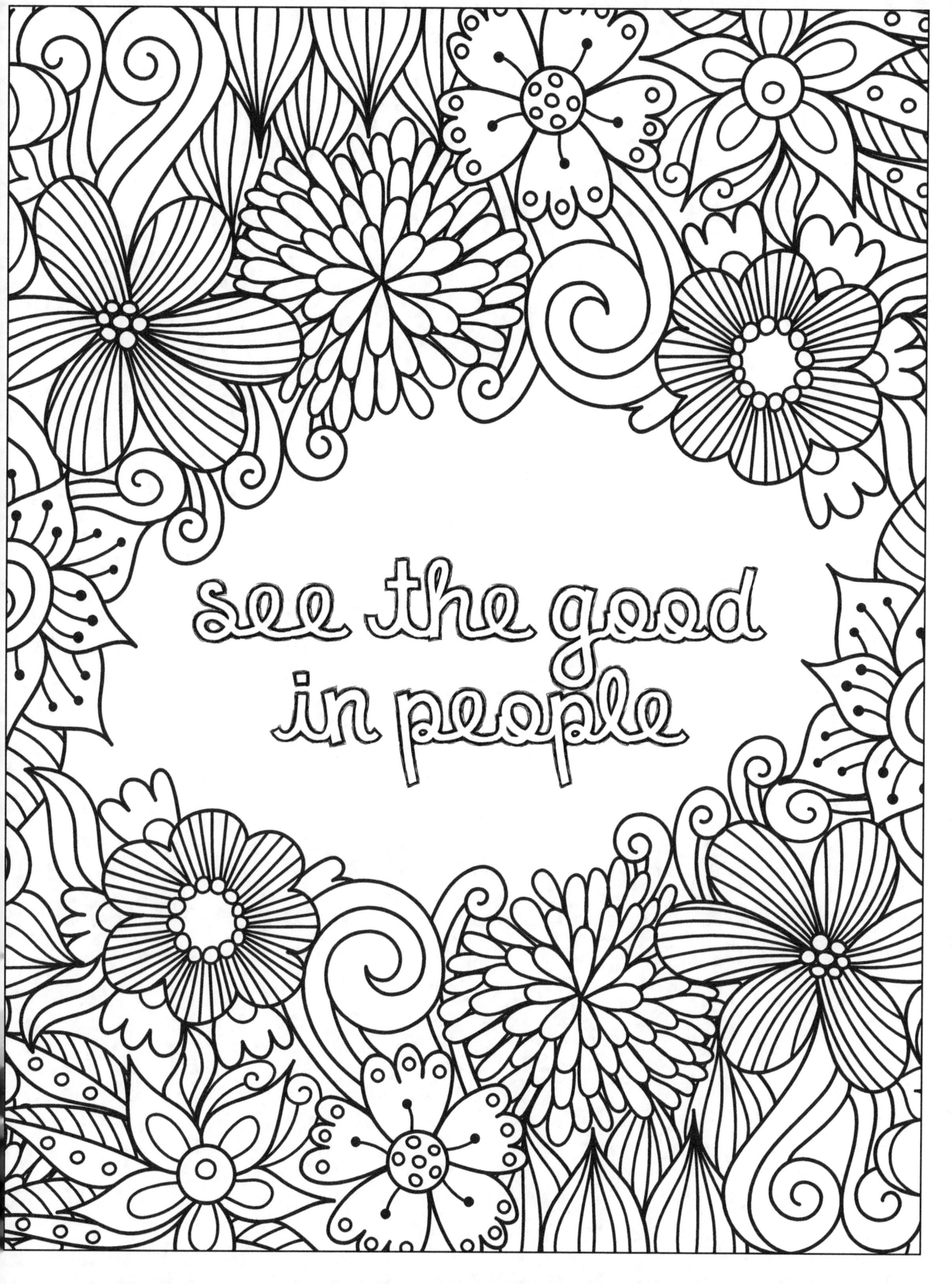

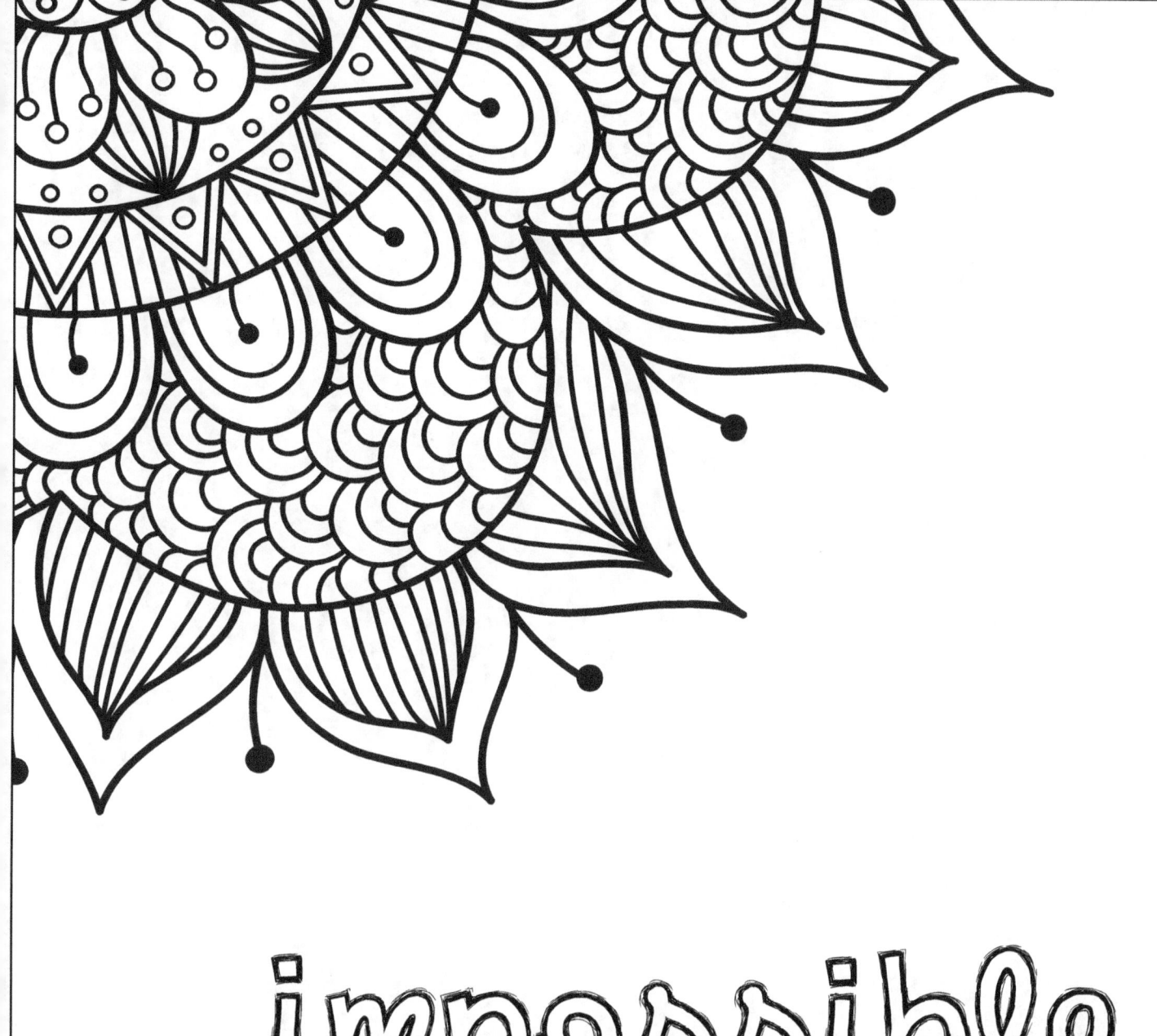

impossible is just an opinion!

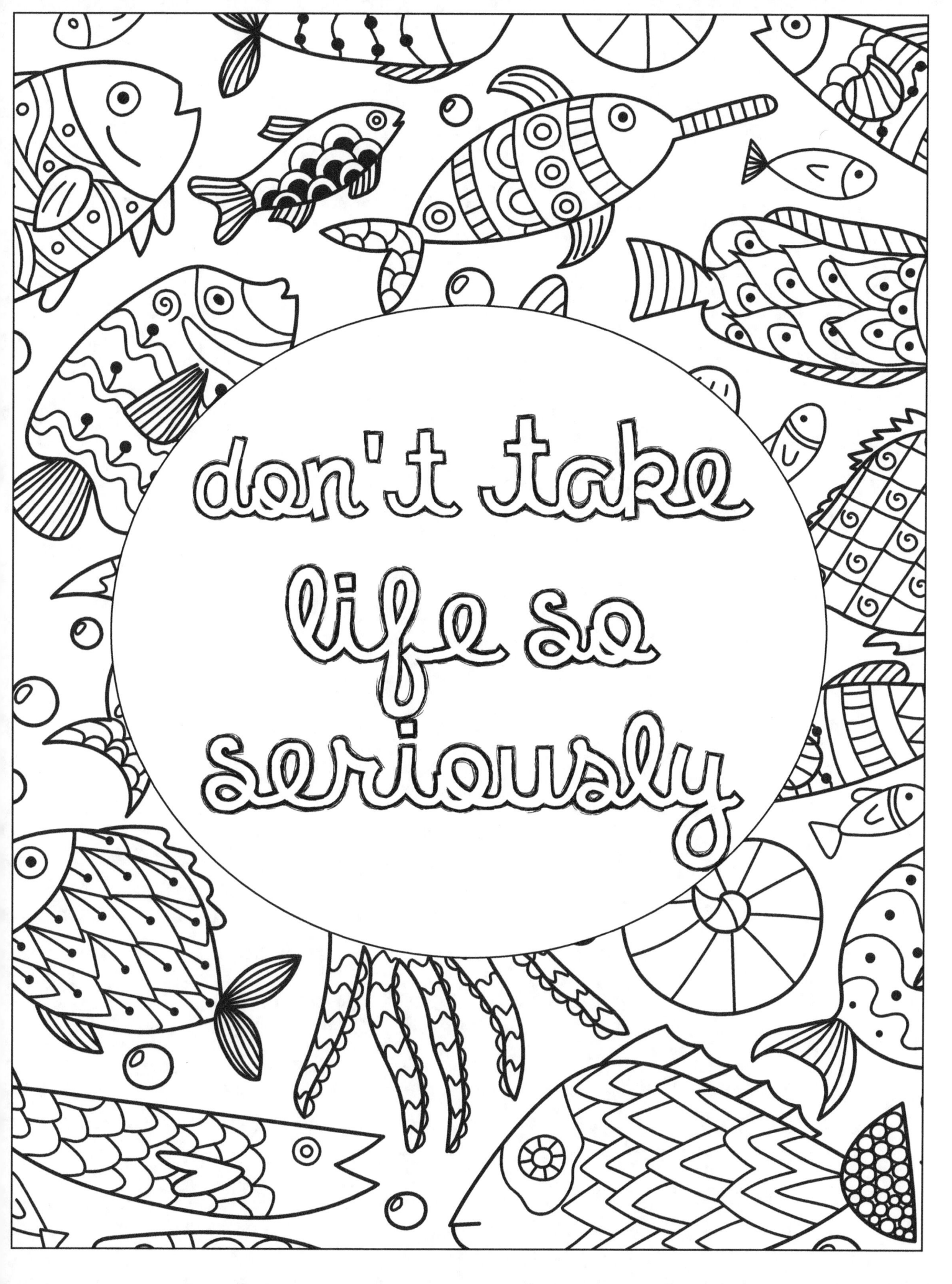

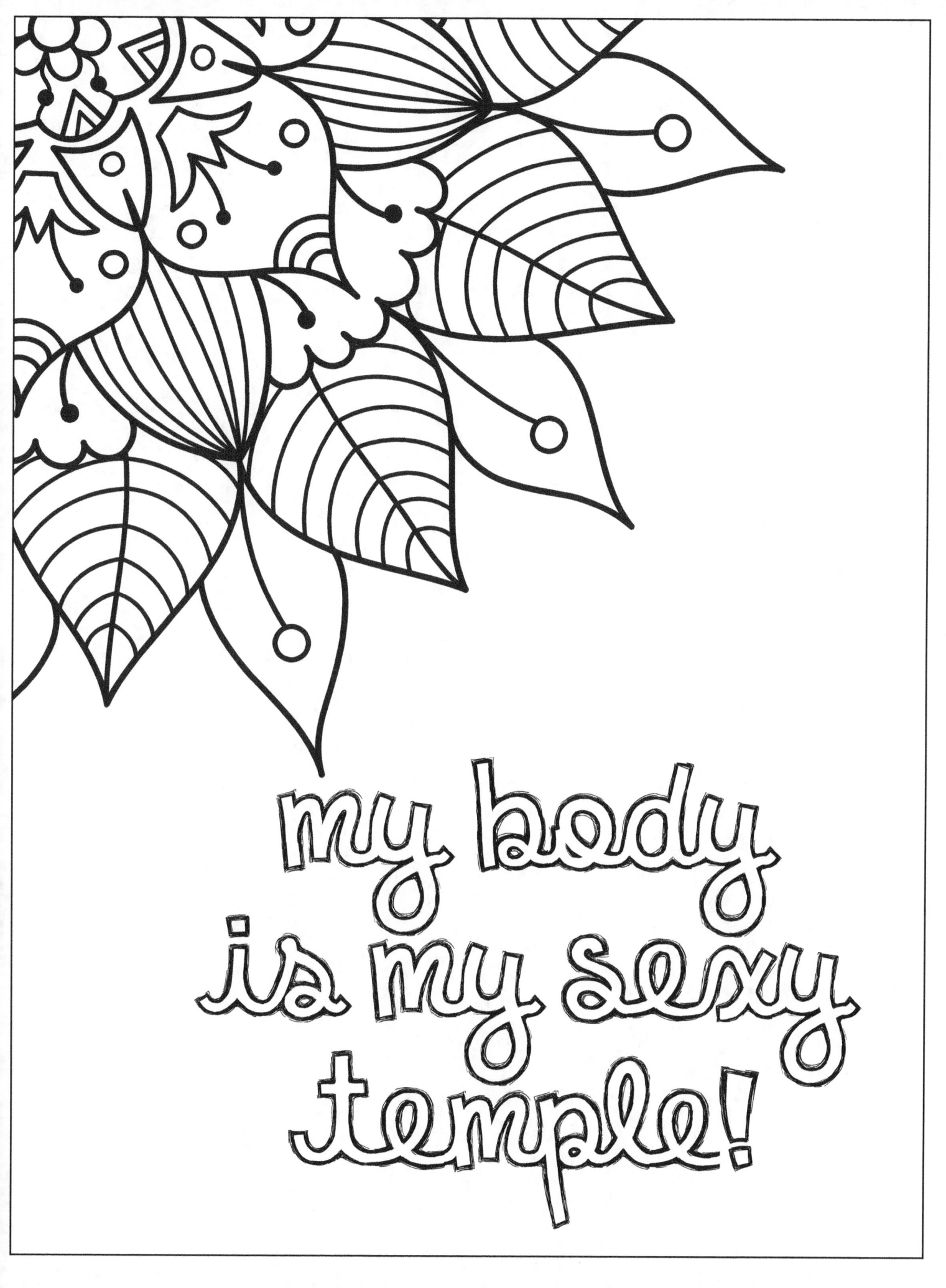

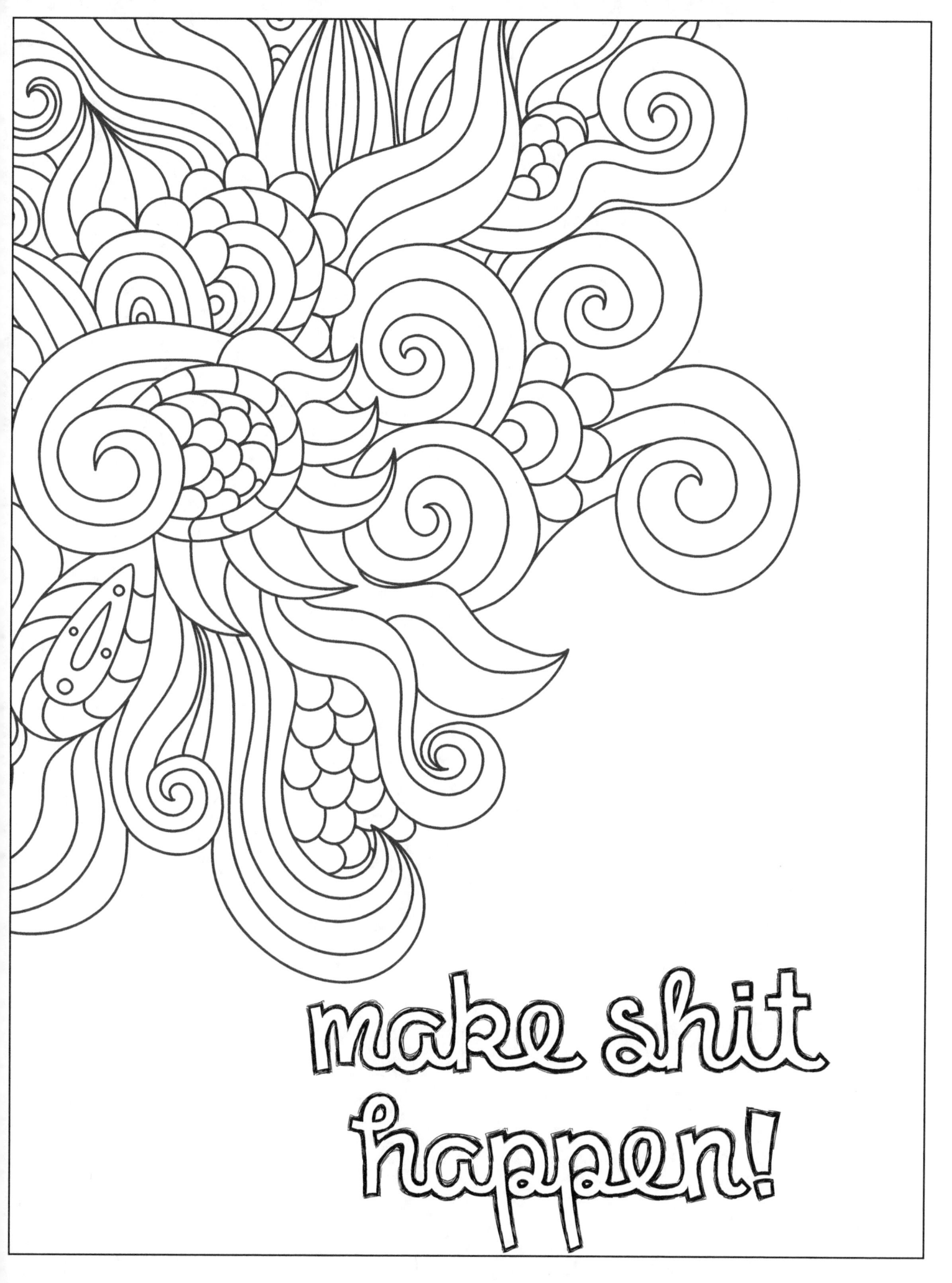

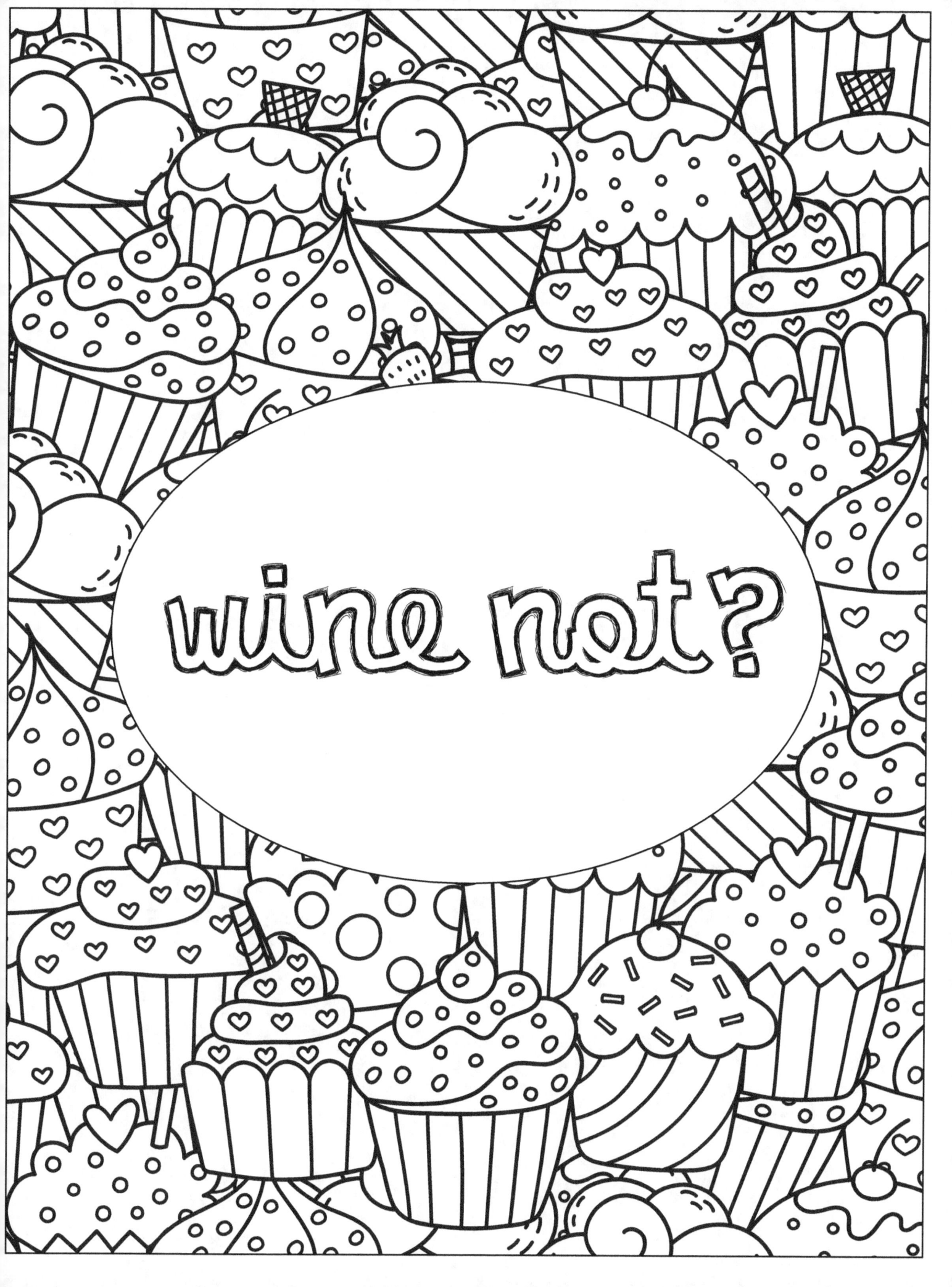

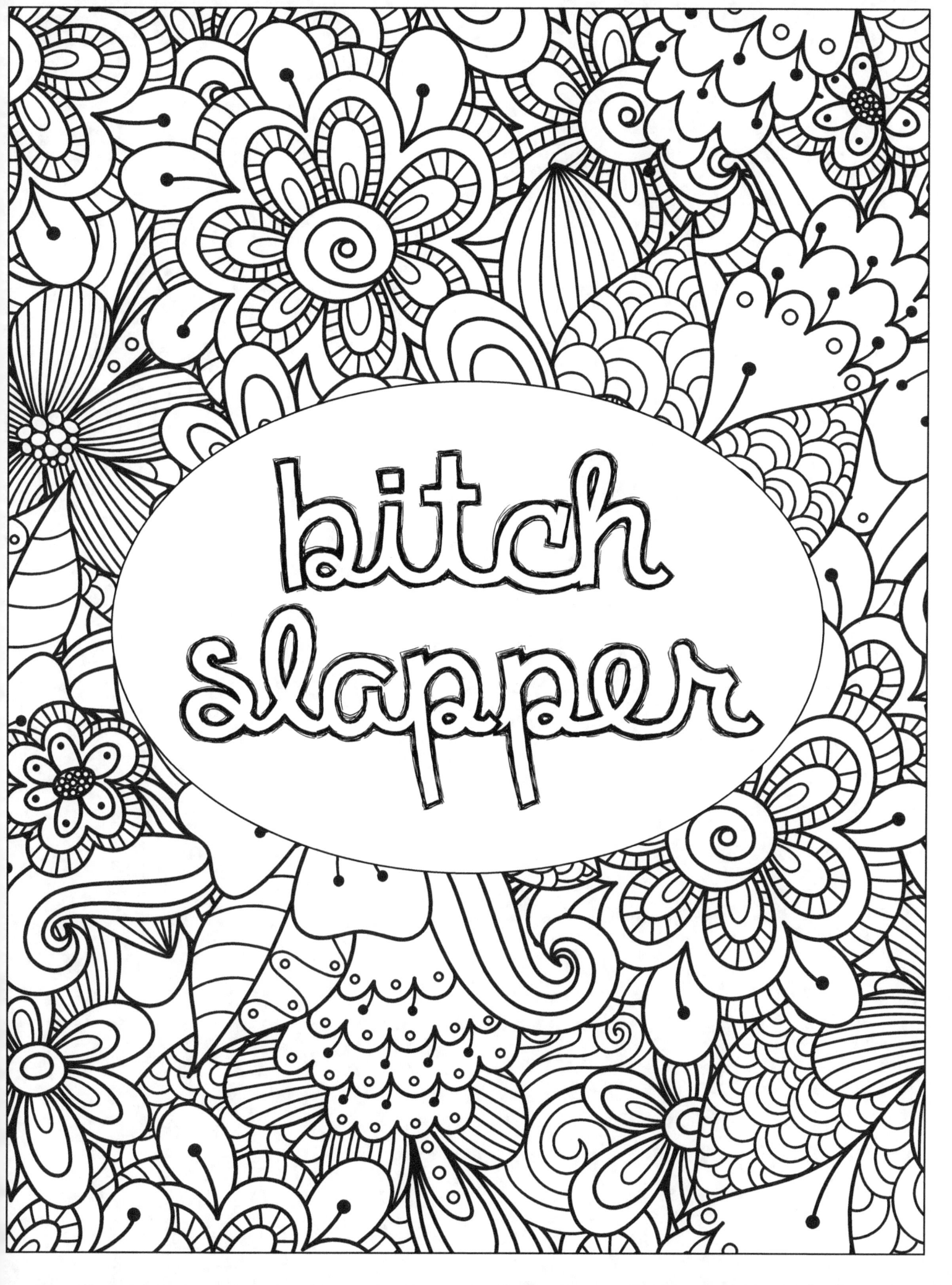

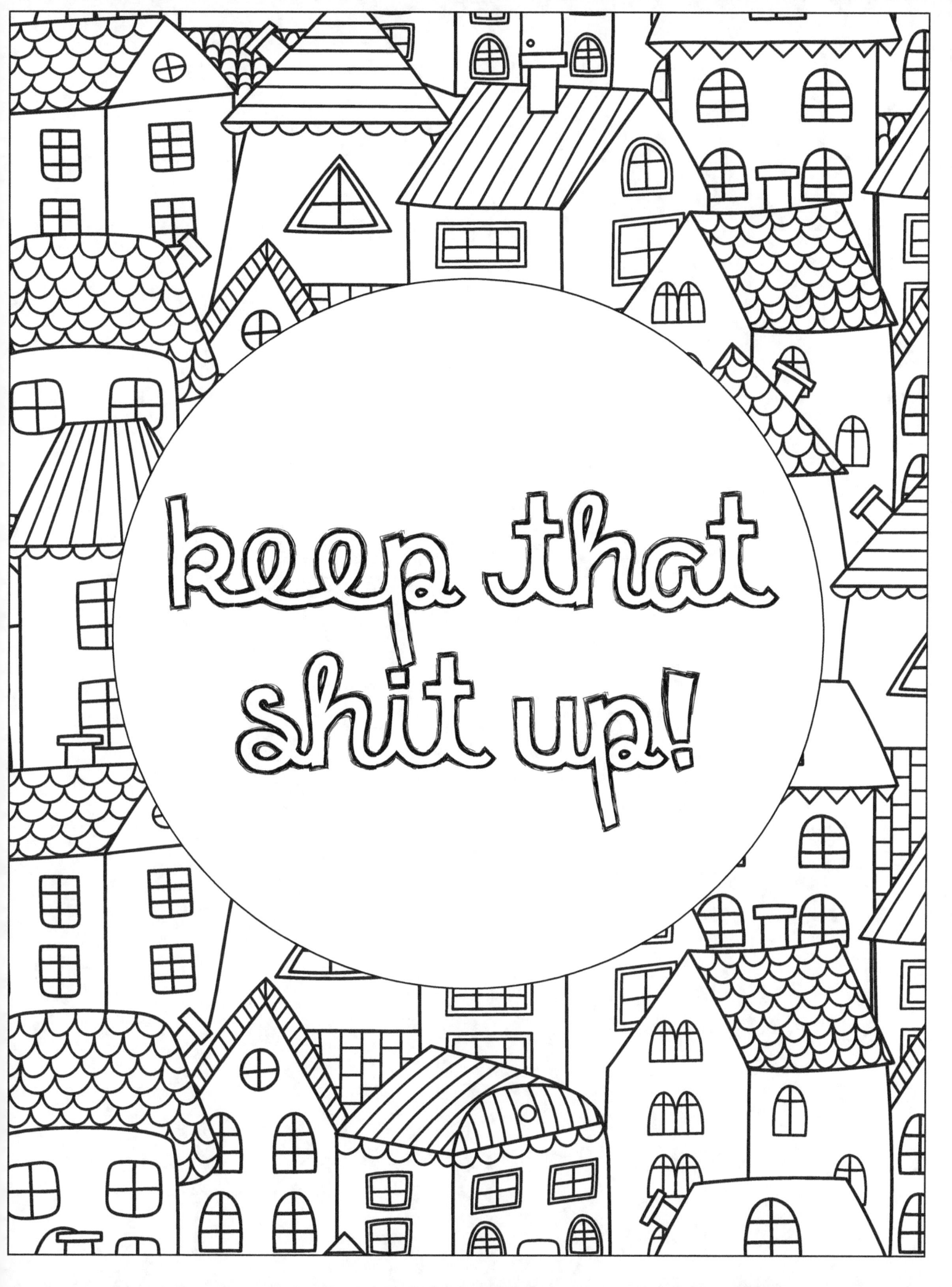

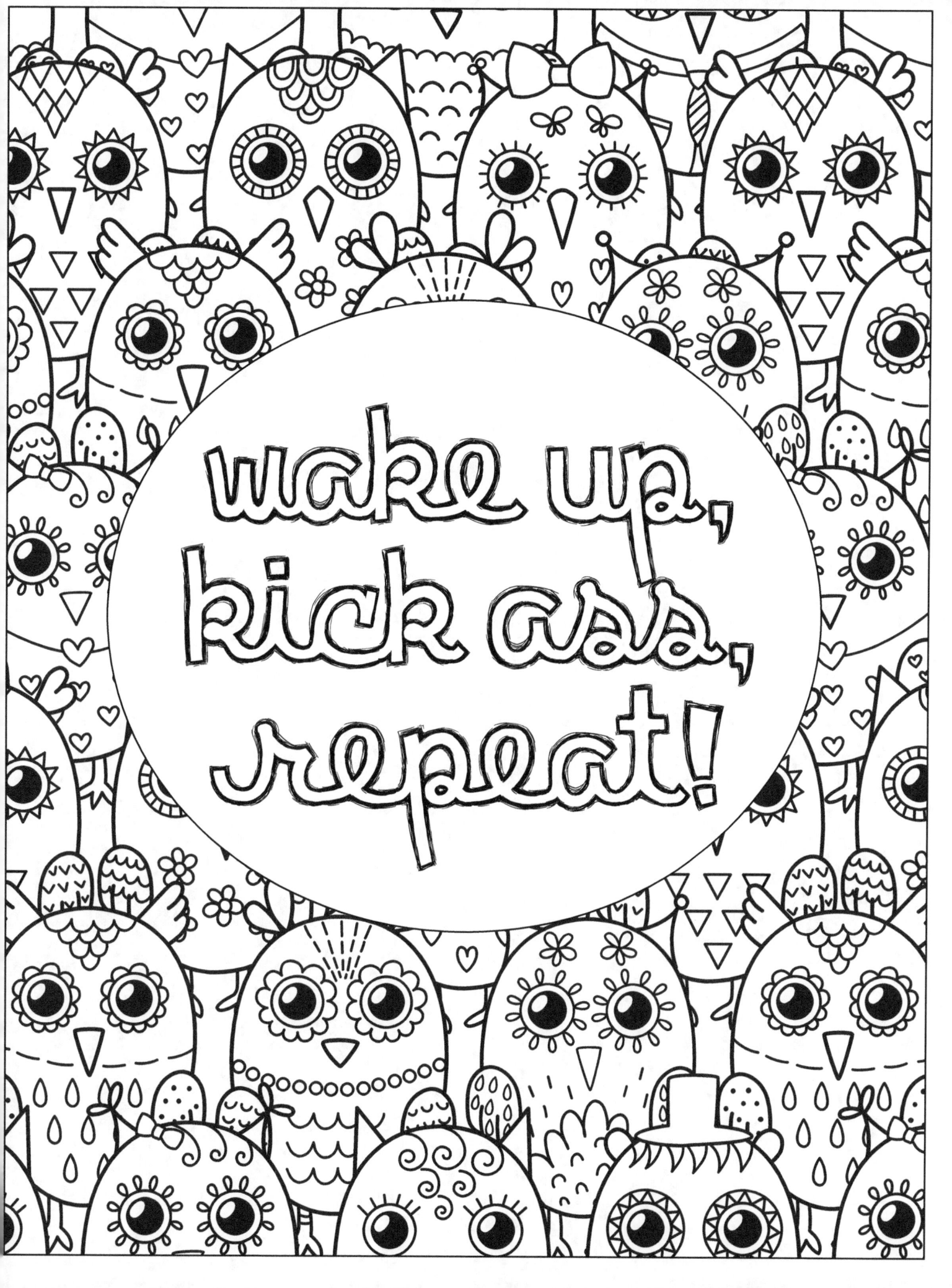

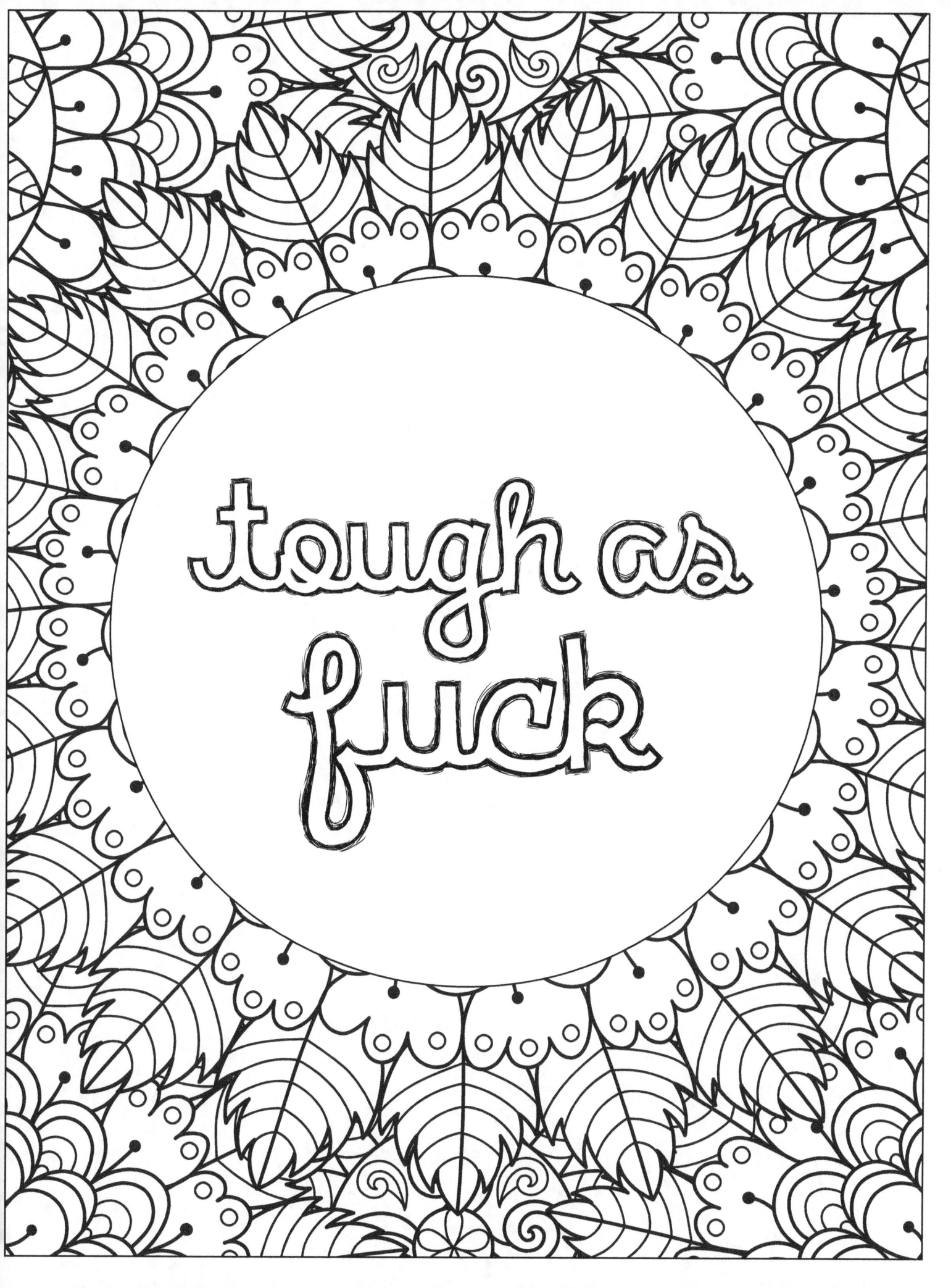

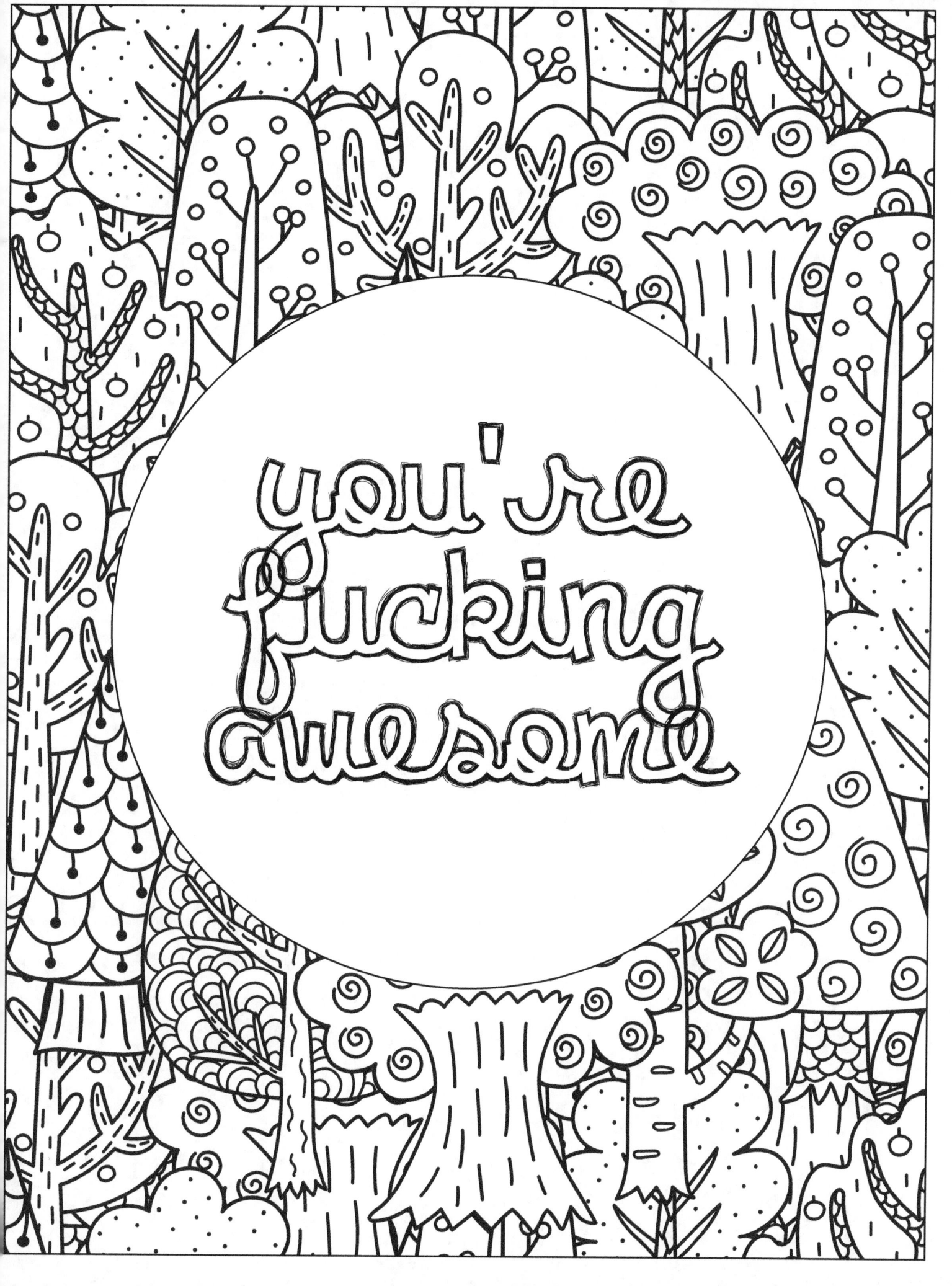

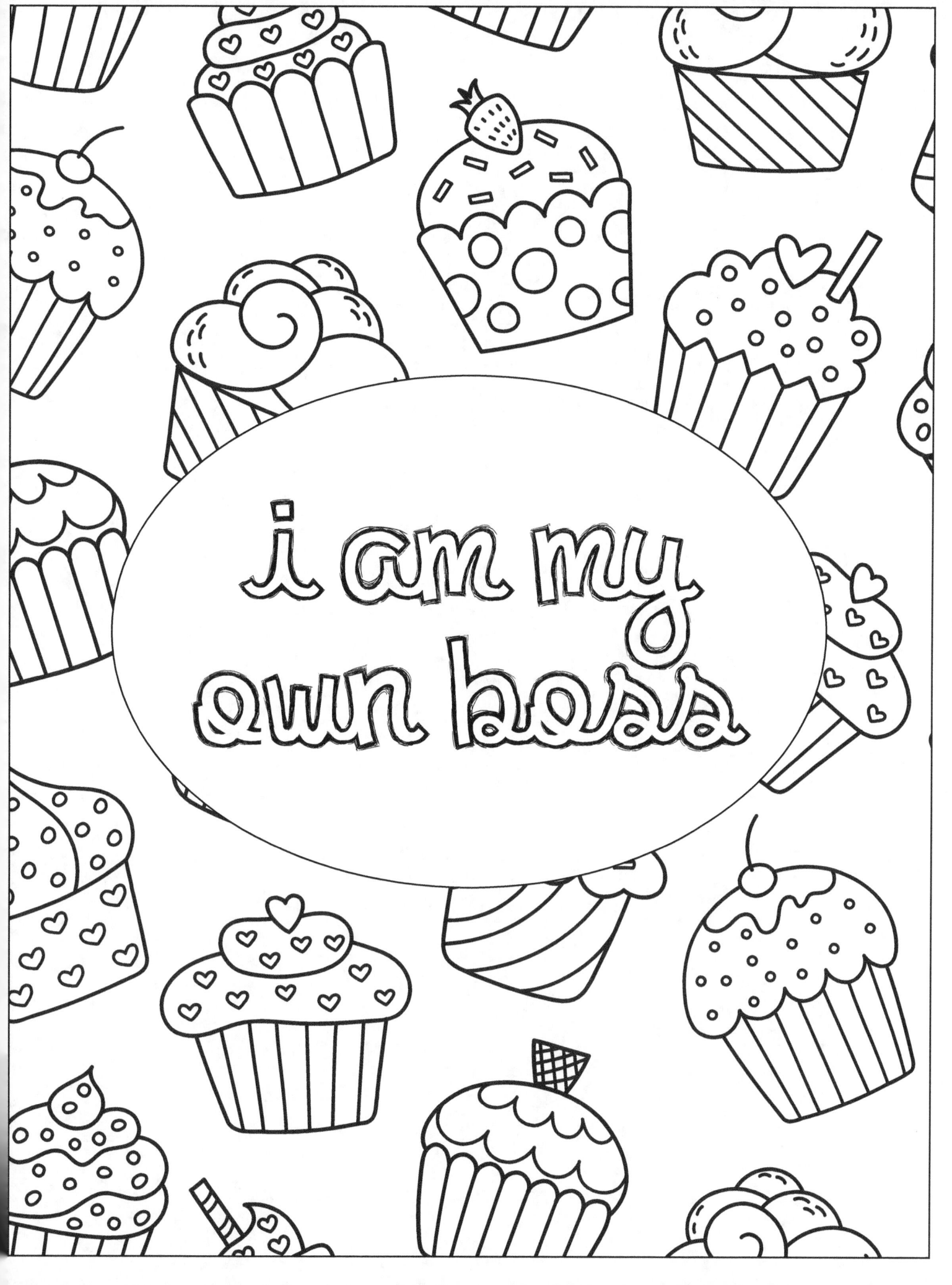

it's been a long trip

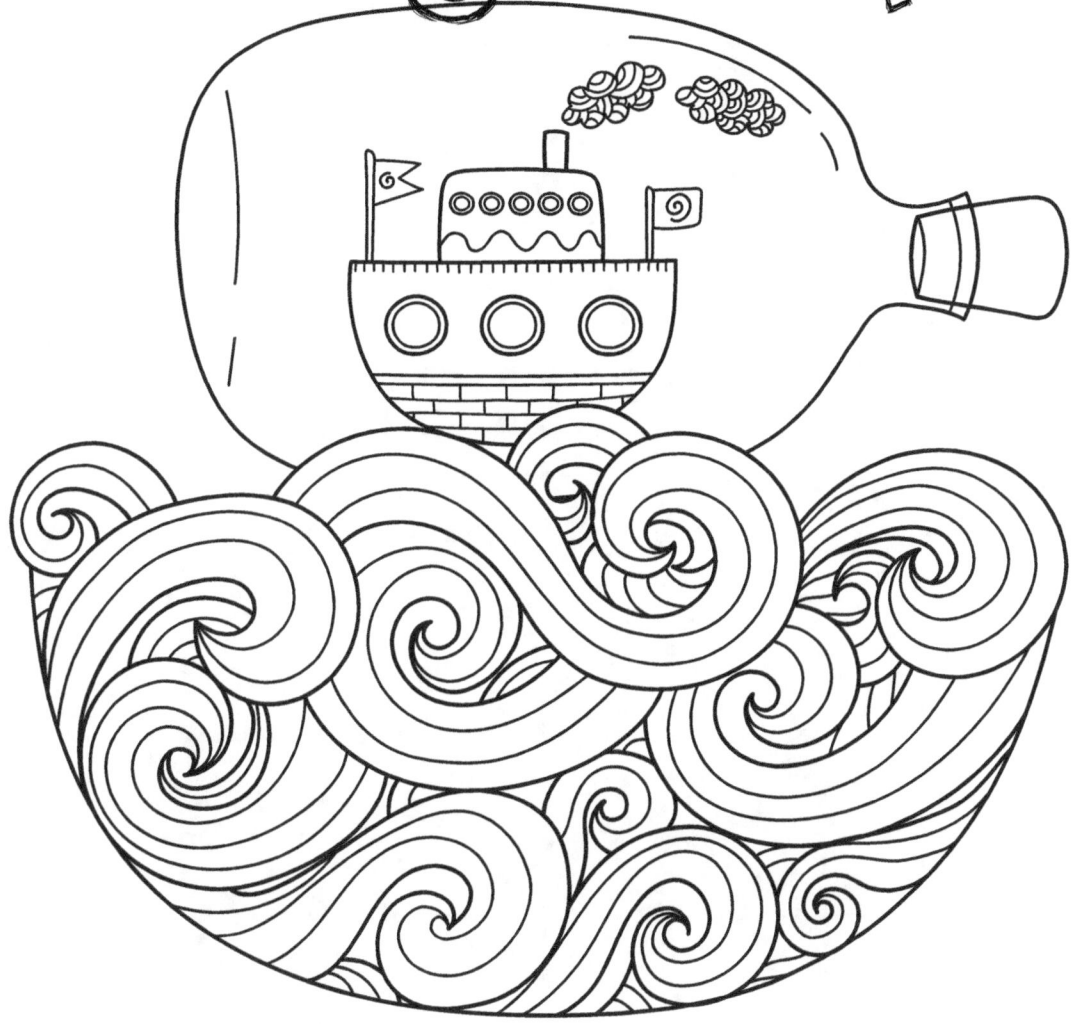

it's called life

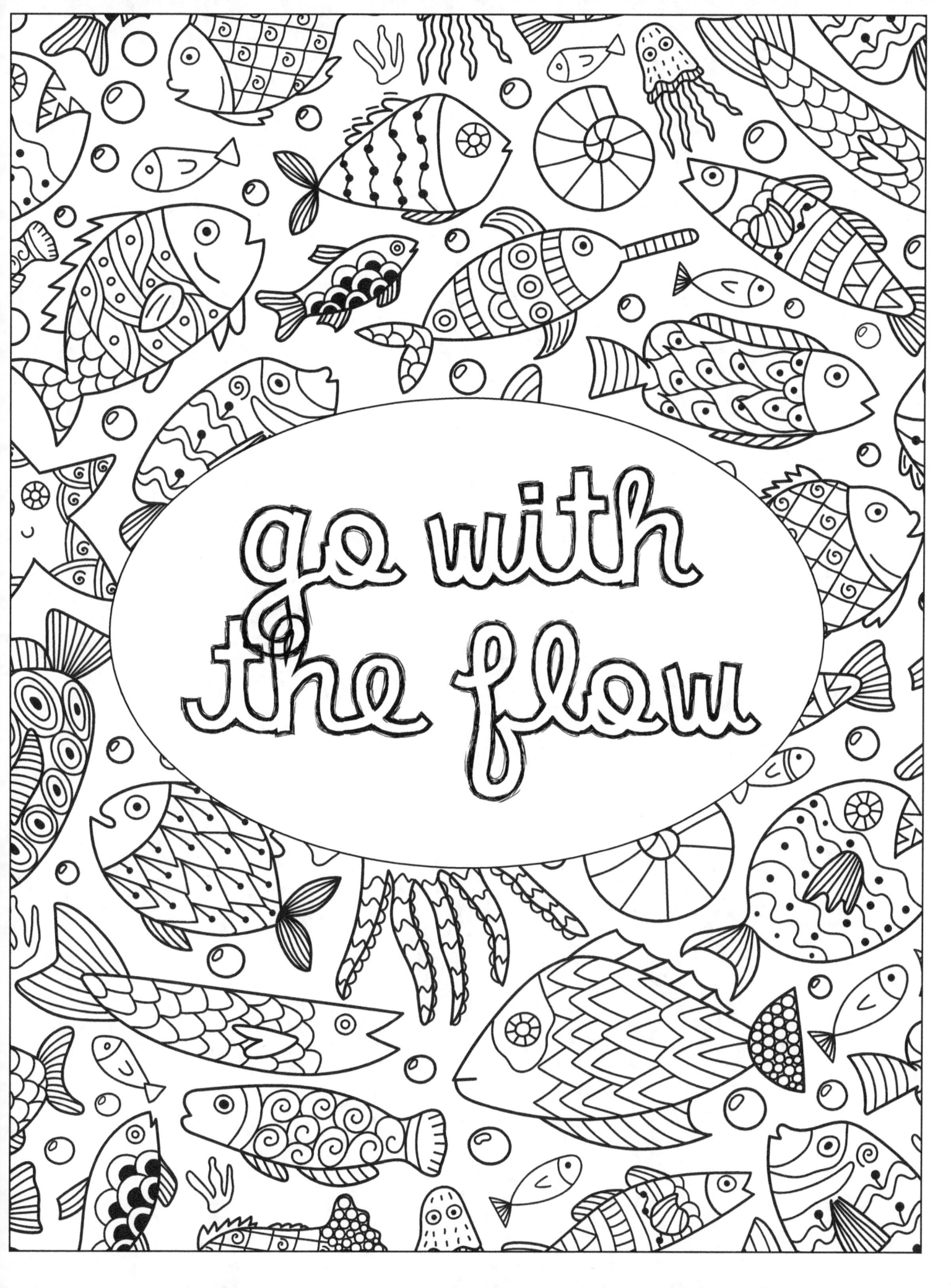

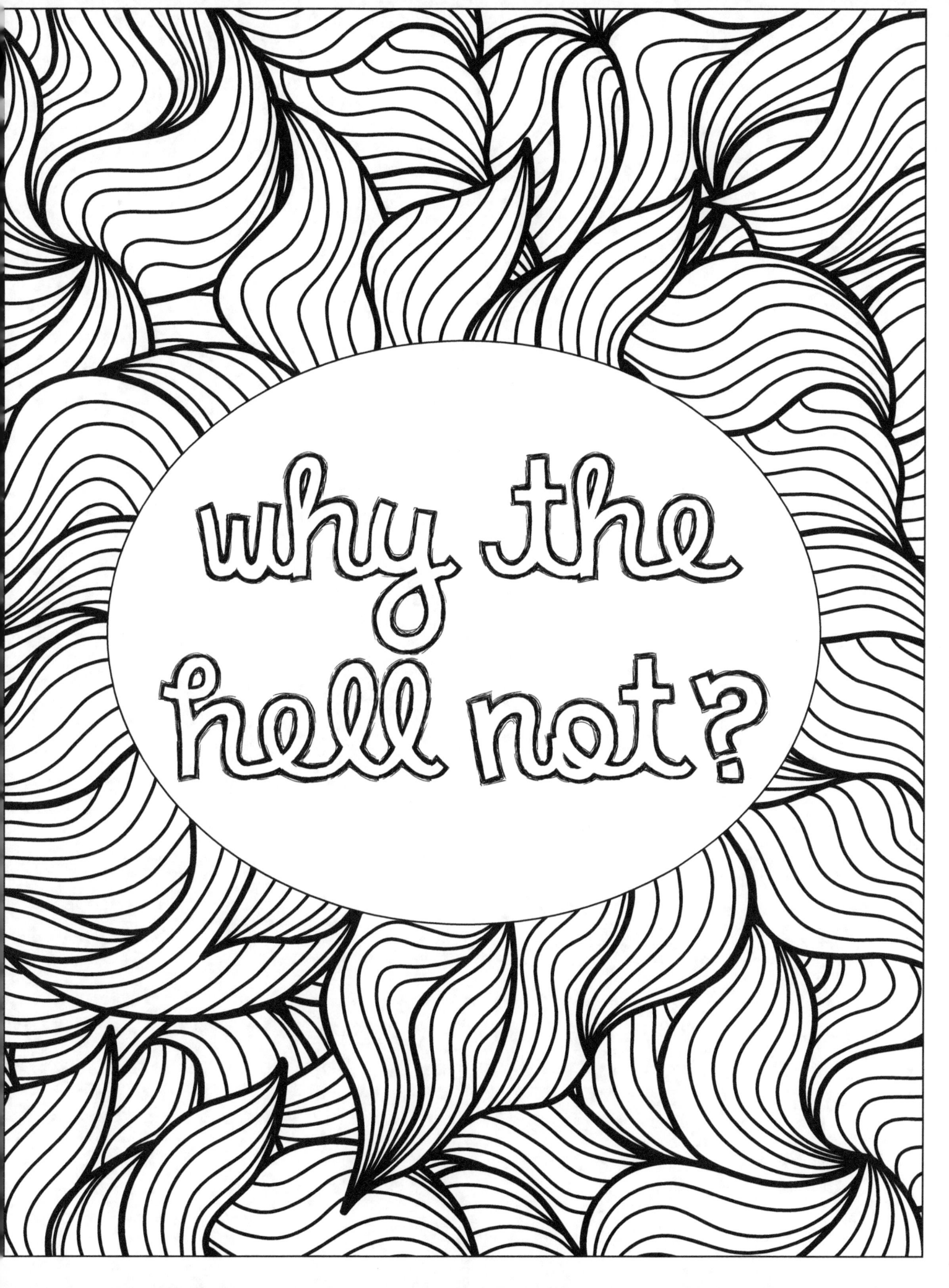

www.ingramcontent.com/pod-product-compliance
Lightning Source LLC
Chambersburg PA
CBHW080230180526

45158CB00009BB/2676